07/20

# WHEN YOUR FRIEND IS SAD

BY ALLAN MOREY

D1199904

BLUE OWL
BOOKS

# TIPS FOR CAREGIVERS

Social and emotional learning (SEL) helps children grow their self and social awareness. They will learn how to manage their emotions and foster empathy toward others. Lessons and support in SEL help children build relationship skills, establish positive habits in communication and cooperation, and make better decisions. By incorporating SEL in early reading, children will have the opportunity to explore different emotions, as well as learn ways to cope with theirs and those of others.

## BEFORE READING

Talk to the reader about feeling sad. Explain that it is an emotion everyone experiences.

**Discuss:** How do you feel when you are sad? How do you act? Do you notice other people acting the same way? Do your friends get sad for the same reasons?

## AFTER READING

Talk to the reader about how to recognize when someone else is sad.

**Discuss:** How can you tell when a friend is sad? What should you do and say? What can you do to help a friend overcome his or her feelings of sadness?

## SEL GOAL

Young students struggle to understand their own emotions, and it can be even more difficult for them to recognize how someone else is feeling. Being able to spot clues in a friend's body language and actions will help improve their social awareness skills. Lead a discussion about how the students react when they are sad. By sharing this information with each other, students can learn how to communicate with a friend or peer who might be feeling sad.

# TABLE OF CONTENTS

# CHAPTER 1

# RECOGNIZING SADNESS

What do we look like when we are sad? We frown. Our upper eyelids droop down. We might **pout**.

We also show sadness with **body language**. These are movements we make that can show how we feel. When sad, we often look down. We might **slouch** our shoulders or cross our arms.

People may speak differently when sad. A friend might talk softly or slowly. Or he mumbles and is hard to understand. Crying is another sign of sadness.

# CHAPTER 2

# UNDERSTANDING SADNESS

We all get sad for different reasons. It can be hard to understand why others are sad. Think. What makes you sad? How do you feel when you are sad? Does this help you understand someone else's feelings?

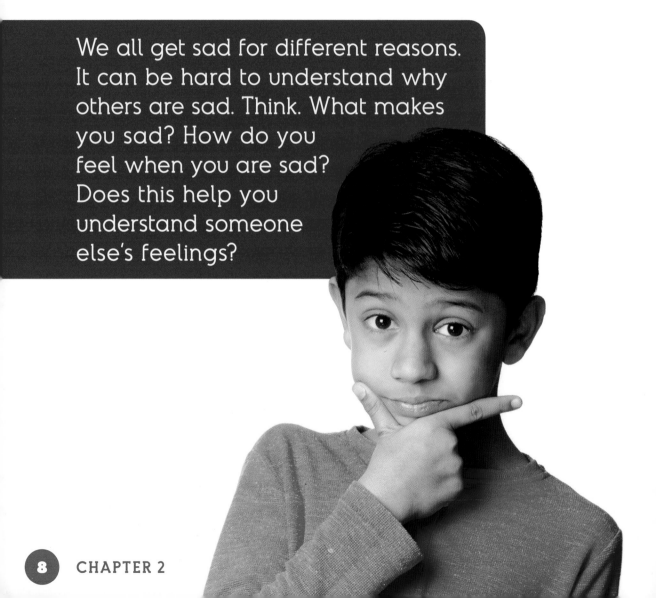

Ann feels down because she got a bad grade at school. Another friend is **upset** because he lost a game. People can also get sad while watching sad movies.

We all need different things when we're sad. One friend wants to be by herself. Why? She doesn't want anyone to see her cry. But Jay likes to have people close. A hug makes him feel better.

## ALONE TIME

Wanting to be alone does not always mean someone is sad. Some people like alone time. Or maybe they do not like big crowds. Look for other signs to know if a friend is truly sad.

Sometimes there are bigger reasons for feeling sad. A friend might be getting bullied. Jake is sad because his best friend moved away.

Your friend could be experiencing **grief**. Maybe her grandmother died.

## DEPRESSION

**Depression** is an intense feeling of sadness that doesn't seem to go away. It causes people to lose interest in things they once enjoyed. They might feel tired all the time. Talk to a trusted adult if you think a friend is experiencing depression.

# CHAPTER 3

# RESPONDING TO SADNESS

You can help a friend who is sad! How? Start by finding out what is wrong. Ask, "Are you OK?" Or, "Do you want to talk?" If your friend does not feel like talking, just wait. Give her time.

Your friend might want to be left alone. That is OK. He could be embarrassed by his **emotions**. Respect his wishes. But say, "I am here if you want to talk."

When your friend wants to talk, just listen. Pay attention. Look at him while he speaks. Don't tell him he shouldn't feel sad. Don't say things like, "It's not that bad." Let him talk about how he feels. Talking can help your friend feel better.

You probably can't fix why a friend is sad. But you can help her feel better. Show her that you care. Make her a card. You could offer her a hug or put your arm around her.

## TALK ABOUT IT

A trusted adult can also help. Sometimes this is a parent or teacher. Sometimes a **counselor** is the best person. Counselors are trained to help us **cope** with emotions.

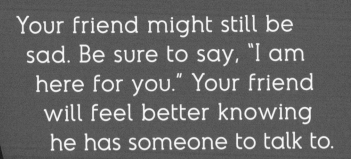

Your friend might still be sad. Be sure to say, "I am here for you." Your friend will feel better knowing he has someone to talk to.

Helping a friend is **rewarding**. Your friend will feel comforted, and you will feel good knowing that you helped. Talking to a friend may even help you understand your own emotions! What will you do the next time your friend is sad?

# GOALS AND TOOLS

## GROW WITH GOALS

Everyone gets sad for different reasons. How can you bring yourself and others joy?

**Goal:** Think happy thoughts! What are some things that make you happy? Think about them when you start to feel sad. What about them makes you happy?

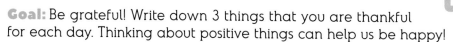

**Goal:** Be grateful! Write down 3 things that you are thankful for each day. Thinking about positive things can help us be happy!

**Goal:** Help a friend who is sad! Ask what is wrong and how you can help. If you know of something that friend likes, help him or her experience it to find joy.

## WRITING REFLECTION

Think about a book you read, a movie you watched, or a song you heard that made you feel sad.

1. Write down what made you sad about the book, movie, or song.

2. Did you still like it, even though it was sad? Why or why not?

3. Then write about the reasons someone might write a sad book, make a sad movie, or sing a sad song.

## GLOSSARY

**body language**
The gestures, movements, and mannerisms by which people communicate with others.

**cope**
To deal with something effectively.

**counselor**
Someone trained to help with problems or give advice.

**depression**
A medical condition in which you feel unhappy or hopeless and can't concentrate or sleep well.

**emotions**
Feelings, such as happiness, anger, or sadness.

**grief**
A feeling of great sadness or deep distress.

**pout**
To push out your lips to express annoyance or disappointment.

**rewarding**
Offering or bringing satisfaction.

**slouch**
To droop or bend forward.

**upset**
Disturbed or very unhappy.

## TO LEARN MORE

**FACT SURFER**

### Finding more information is as easy as 1, 2, 3.

1. Go to www.factsurfer.com

2. Enter "**whenyourfriendissad**" into the search box.

3. Choose your cover to see a list of websites.

# INDEX

Blue Owl Books are published by Jump!, 5357 Penn Avenue South, Minneapolis, MN 55419, www.jumplibrary.com

Copyright © 2020 Jump! International copyright reserved in all countries. No part of this book may be reproduced in any form without written permission from the publisher.

Library of Congress Cataloging-in-Publication Data

Names: Morey, Allan, author.
Title: When your friend is sad / Allan Morey.
Description: MN: Jump!, Inc., [2020] | Series: You've got a friend
Includes index. | Audience: Ages 7–10 | Audience: Grades 2-3
Identifiers: LCCN 2019036689 (print)
LCCN 2019036690 (ebook)
ISBN 9781645272175 (hardcover)
ISBN 9781645272182 (paperback)
ISBN 9781645272199 (ebook)
Subjects: LCSH: Sadness in children—Juvenile literature.
Empathy in children—Juvenile literature. | Friendship—Juvenile literature.
Classification: LCC BF723.S15 M67 2020 (print)
LCC BF723.S15 (ebook) | DDC 152.4—dc23
LC record available at https://lccn.loc.gov/2019036689
LC ebook record available at https://lccn.loc.gov/2019036690

Editor: Susanne Bushman
Designer: Molly Ballanger

Photo Credits: ti-ja/iStock, cover; Zdravinjo/Shutterstock, 1; kwanchai.c/Shutterstock, 3; sunabesyou/Shutterstock, 4; Pressmaster/Shutterstock, 5; Lapina/Shutterstock, 6–7; saisnaps/Shutterstock, 8; Urilux/iStock, 9; vernonwiley/iStock, 10–11; Africa Studio/Shutterstock, 12 (background); kali9/iStock, 12 (framed image); Blue_Cutler/iStock, 14; BUNDITINAY/Shutterstock, 15; Veja/Shutterstock, 16–17; FatCamera/iStock, 18–19; monkeybusinessimages/iStock, 20–21; Ljupco Smokovski/Shutterstock, 23.

Printed in the United States of America at Corporate Graphics in North Mankato, Minnesota.